ROLLING DREAMS
Portraits of the Northwest's Railroad Heritage

Text and Photography by

D. C. JESSE BURKHARDT

Copyright © 1997 by D. C. Jesse Burkhardt
ISBN 0-9661042-7-7

COVER:
"WATER COLORS"
Burlington Northern Santa Fe Railway
Fallbridge Subdivision
Columbia River Gorge
April 16, 1997

ROLLING DREAMS:
All photos by D. C. Jesse Burkhardt, except where indicated
Graphic Design: Micki Chapman/Relative Design, Hood River, Oregon
Color scans/film: Wy'east Color Inc., Portland, Oregon
Printing: Dynagraphics, Portland, Oregon

ISBN 0-9661042-7-7
Copyright © 1997
"Rolling Dreams"
P.O. Box 1054
White Salmon, Washington 98672

Also by D. C. Jesse Burkhardt:
Backwoods Railroads: Branchlines and Shortlines of Western Oregon
(ISBN: 0-87422-104-8)
WSU Press: 1-800-354-7360

One of the books that became something of a spiritual guide during the creation of *Rolling Dreams* was Michael Flanagan's wonderful *Stations: An Imagined Journey*, published by Pantheon in 1994. Flanagan's vision blurred the edges between photography and artwork, and the inspiration gleaned from that work helped to drive this project. Two other inspiring books: *Reaching Home: Pacific Salmon, Pacific People,* by Natalie Fobes, which Alaska Northwest Books released in 1994; and Greg McDonnell's *Heartland,* published in 1993 by Boston Mills Press.

CONTENTS

INTRODUCTION..3

I. ON THE MAINLINE:
   Tracks Through the Columbia River Gorge...................17

II. NOTHING BUT THE RAILS: Branchlines and Shortlines................33

III. THE UNHEEDED ROUTES: Northwest Images...............59

IV. DONE IN PASTELS: Dispatches..81

V. ADDENDUM: Michigan Roots...83

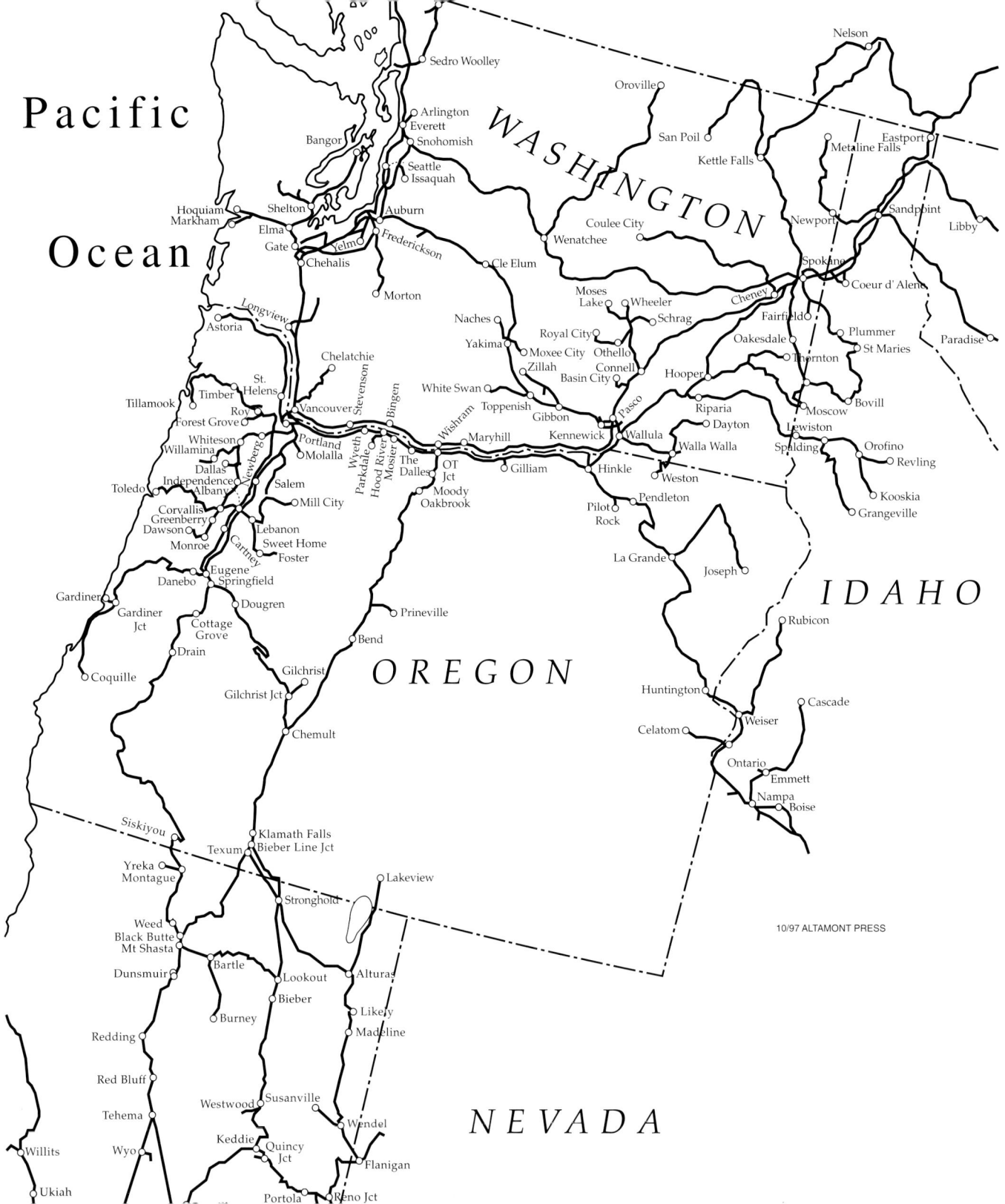

"WRENS TURN"
Southern Pacific Railroad
Toledo Branch
Corvallis Junction, Oregon
May 1991

INTRODUCTION

It's amazing how suddenly everything shifted. Until the mid-1980s, the major railroads were holding on to most of their branchlines. Except for the occasional abandonment of aging, unprofitable lines without high-volume shippers, the big Western carriers — Southern Pacific, Union Pacific, Burlington Northern — continued to send trains into the rustic landscapes of the Northwest to pick up two or three hoppers at an isolated grain elevator; continued to venture far from the hustling metropolitan hubs to pick up a flatcar or two of lumber at a backwoods sawmill.

When Washington State University Press published my first book, *Backwoods Railroads: Branchlines and Shortlines of Western Oregon*, in June 1994, the rail transportation network in the Pacific Northwest was changing so quickly it proved difficult to set a rational stopping point for the work. Holding its publication until 1994 proved to be auspicious timing, however, because there were dramatic shifts in the Northwest's railroad network in 1993-94 — shifts that would alter the railroad landscape forever.

By the end of 1994, Southern Pacific Transportation Company's remaining Oregon branchlines had been axed, concluding a trend ongoing for a number of years. The process began in earnest in February 1993, as SP shed the West Side Branch, Bailey Branch, Toledo Branch, and segments of the Newberg Branch, all of which went to the fledgling Willamette & Pacific Railroad. At the same time, the Molalla Branch was sold to the Molalla Western Railway. Then, SP's Geer Branch and Stayton Branch were leased to the Willamette Valley Railroad.

And the changes didn't end there.

On December 31, 1994, SP's Coos Bay Line and the storied Siskiyou Line were handed over to the newly-created Central Oregon & Pacific Railroad. CO&P bought most of the 300-mile Siskiyou Line outright, and signed a lease to operate the entire 138-mile Coos Bay Line. The $18 million transaction pulled another 438 miles out of the SP system. It also brought local management of the two rural lines closer to home, because while Southern Pacific was based in San Francisco, CO&P located its headquarters on the Siskiyou Line in Roseburg, Oregon — at the heart of one of the state's most intensive lumber-producing regions.

SP's plan to drop its anemic feeder lines was aggressive. In 1990, SP owned and operated more than 700 miles of branchlines in Oregon. By the beginning of 1995, SP operated essentially none.

Union Pacific was busily engaged in line spin-offs as well, selling its 84-mile Joseph Branch (between La Grande and Joseph, Oregon) to the Idaho Northern & Pacific Railroad in November 1993. The

"SECTION CREW"
Spokane, Portland & Seattle Railway
Stevenson, Washington
1908
Photo courtesy of Burlington Northern Santa Fe Railway; collection of Gus Melonas

The way it began: Track Foreman Gust Melonas (third from left) with all-Greek section crew at Stevenson, Washington. This crew was involved with the original SP&S construction project that built — with picks and shovels — the first rail line through the Columbia River Gorge. Melonas also served as general foreman on the construction of the Oregon Trunk route. James J. Hill, the first president of the Great Northern Railway, ate Greek food with Melonas' crews on more than one occasion.

"TURNTABLE"
Southern Pacific Railroad
Tillamook Branch
Timber, Oregon
Winter 1946
Photo by Ed Maas; collection of Tom Dill

Southern Pacific locomotive #2742 gets a spin on the turntable at Timber, Oregon, in 1946. In only a few years, what now appears commonplace may be just as rare.

"FLAGSHIP"
Willamette Valley Railroad
SW1200 #201 (ex-Southern Pacific #2273)
Independence, Oregon
January 26, 1990

Idaho Northern & Pacific bought three other UP branches as well, all of them in western Idaho: Nampa to Cascade, Payette to Emmett, and Weiser to Rubicon — in combination, about 295 miles.

Similar events were taking place in Washington. Significant alterations to the transportation map included Burlington Northern Santa Fe selling off its 134-mile Oroville to Wenatchee line to the Cascade & Columbia River Railroad on September 9, 1996. The Cascade & Columbia diverts from BNSF's Scenic Subdivision mainline at Olds Junction, near Wenatchee. The route appears to be fairly healthy: BN reported that it moved 7,000 carloads over the line in 1995.

In April 1996, BNSF decided that it wanted to sell 277 miles of track in eastern Washington and northern Idaho as part of what it referred to as its continuing asset evaluation program. Included in the sale package were its Palouse lines, with branches from Marshall, Washington, to Arrow, Idaho (122 miles, although the line east of Moscow, Idaho, was out of service); and the line from Palouse, Washington, to Bovill, Idaho (47 miles), where it connected with Idaho's St. Maries River Railroad. BNSF also put up for sale its 108-mile route from Cheney to Coulee City, Washington. On September 6, 1996, all three lines went to the new Palouse River & Coulee City Railroad, which was created by the same owners who controlled the Blue Mountain Railroad and the Palouse River Railroad.

Union Pacific had made its moves in the Palouse area a few years earlier. In November 1992, UP sold or leased several southeastern Washington branchlines to the Palouse River Railroad. Included in the transaction were UP's Palouse region grain branches between Hooper Junction and Colfax, Washington (53 miles); between Winona and Thornton, Washington (32 miles); and between Colfax and Moscow, Idaho (29 miles).

Another four lines radiating out of Walla Walla were transferred to the Blue Mountain Railroad. These routes went northeast to Dayton (38 miles); east to Walair (4 miles); south to Weston, Oregon (26 miles); and west 31 miles to Wallula Junction.

Locomotives seen on the three Palouse-area shortlines include a diversity of origins, with units formerly rostered by the Ohio Central Railroad (GP30), CSX (GP30), Conrail (GP30 and GP35), South Kansas & Oklahoma (GP30), and Eastern Idaho Railroad (GP7) on the job.

Steve Kahler, general manager of the Blue Mountain Railroad explained that the carriers usually don't have any regularly scheduled operations.

"There are not daily runs per se," Kahler said. "We run on demand to meet our customers' needs. But we're going in one direction or the other daily, five days a week. Business is pretty good. We're moving a lot of grain right now. That's the biggest commodity."

"HARVEST WAIT"
Palouse River Railroad
Tekoa Subdivision
Hooper, Washington
December 1996

The mega-carriers readily acknowledged the advantages a shortline railroad could provide.

"The local focus of a short line allows it to remain in very close contact with shippers, which often translates into service better tailored to customers' specific needs," explained Doug Babb, BNSF's senior vice president and chief of staff. "Also, a shortline operator's reduced cost structure can create opportunities for traffic growth at reduced costs for shippers. This can improve the chances of long-term viability on a marginal line."

An example of the opportunity for traffic growth was provided by the Willamette & Pacific. According to W&P business records, the shortline was able to substantially boost the number of carloads of freight generated as opposed to what Southern Pacific had done in recent years. In the last full year that SP ran trains on its western Oregon branchlines (1992), the carrier hauled 28,900 carloads of freight. In 1994, W&P's first complete year of handling service on the same lines, W&P moved 35,210 carloads — a jump of more than 6,300 cars in less than two years. In 1995, the figure was basically stable, with 35,150 cars handled. In 1996, W&P boosted the figure to 39,322 cars.

Dick Samuels, owner of the Molalla Western Railroad, had similar success: "In March 1997, we moved 147 cars — that broke all records," Samuels said. "We're double over what we were doing last year."

He pointed out that when Southern Pacific worked the line, it averaged 60 to 70 cars a month.

With all the changes, there was no way to predict what company might be hauling freight around the region from one month to the next. A Burlington Northern branch one week could be a new shortline the next, and instead of BN GP38-2s working, there might instead be ex-Conrail GP40s, or ex-SP SD9s. To confuse things even further, much of the used equipment remained in the original owner's paint, as shortline companies were not likely to invest time and cash on cosmetics. So instead of a fresh paint job, usually the former company's logo would simply be painted over, with perhaps crude stenciling to identify the new company running trains on the line.

The Central Oregon & Pacific provided an appropriate object lesson: The motive power on a southbound *Montague Hauler* leaving Medford, Oregon, on its way to northern California on May 29, 1996, included three different paint schemes — Burlington Northern green, Norfolk Southern black, and Central Oregon & Pacific red. Leading the way in that instance were ex-Burlington Northern GP40 #3076 (with "CORP" stenciled lettering), ex-BN GP40 #3079, ex-Norfolk Southern GP40 #1338, Central Oregon & Pacific GP38 #5533, ex-NS GP40 #1335, and CO&P GP38 #5528. Pushing as helpers at the rear of the train were three more GP38s in CO&P's dark red.

Along with all the fresh railroad companies starting up in the 1990s,

"SANTA FE FLOOD"
Willamette & Pacific Railroad
Newberg District
Middleton, Oregon
July 3, 1994

When the Willamette & Pacific took over branchline operations on several Southern Pacific routes in Oregon in 1993, the carrier brought in a roster of former Santa Fe GP39-2s. Because getting business going was much more important than having a pretty corporate image to flash around the countryside, dressing locomotives in W&P's own paint scheme was secondary to moving trains. As a result, for a short time in 1993, locomotives with the bold, famous "Santa Fe" lettering were seen in Oregon. It was somewhat ironic to see a flood of yellow and blue Santa Fe units moving across Oregon where SP had held sway for decades, given that the proposed merger between SP and SF had fallen apart only seven years earlier. Coming west through Middleton, Oregon, is a Newberg-bound freight headed by three of W&P's ex-Santa Fe GP39-2s: #2308, #2316, and #2302. All the Santa Fe lettering has been painted over.

there were some mothballed lines that returned to work as well. The Klamath Northern Railway, built in 1938, was one of these. Service on the 10.6-mile line between a Gilchrist Lumber Company sawmill at Gilchrist, Oregon, and an interchange with Southern Pacific's Cascade Line at Gilchrist Junction squealed to a halt in 1991. Crown Pacific Ltd. subsequently purchased the sawmill, and reactivated the railroad in December 1994. Part of Crown Pacific's operations required importing logs from New Zealand, which were arriving on American shores at the Port of Coos Bay. Log trains were moving to the Gilchrist mill an average of three or four times a week in 1997, with between 10 and 20 cars in each move.

"There's no set schedule," said Terry Anderson, administrative assistant for the Klamath Northern. "It depends on whether we're getting log imports." She added that the railroad, powered by a single locomotive — Klamath Northern #207, a GE 125T center-cab switcher — also hauls carloads of finished lumber outbound from the mill.

One major carrier in the Northwest provided a dramatic restoration of service over what had been an embargoed route. In 1996, BNSF reopened the former Northern Pacific route across Stampede Pass in Washington's Cascade Range.

After almost 100 years as a primary rail corridor — the line was built in 1887 — a 78-mile segment of the mainline between Auburn and Cle Elum, Washington, had been taken out of service in August 1983 as BN

"BEND LOCAL"
Union Pacific Railroad
SD40-2 #3306/SD40-2 #3781
Deschutes River Canyon
Moody, Oregon
June 14, 1997

shed what it considered at the time to be redundant and unprofitable lines in central Washington. A new shortline called the Washington Central Railroad was created in October 1986 to handle local freight service between Cle Elum and Pasco, Washington. BN's through line across the mountains was basically left to rust, although most of the trackage remained in place. That proved to be fortuitous, because in 1996, the moribund Stampede Pass route experienced a rebirth when BN's traffic planners looked at their system maps, then looked at tracks crowded with too many trains to move efficiently. So for $40 million, BNSF bought out the Washington Central Railroad as part of a strategy to reopen the mainline. On December 7, 1996, the first merchandise train (110 grain cars) in more than a dozen years rolled over the mountain pass.

A similar situation took place in 1995 on a shortline railroad, when the Central Oregon & Pacific reopened the former SP route across the Siskiyou Mountains. SP had mothballed the line in 1992, but on June 5, 1995 — after a two and a half year hiatus — steel wheels rolled through Siskiyou Summit again as a southbound freight headed by five CO&P locomotives carried 14 carloads of plywood from Medford to Montague, California. In Montague, a waiting CO&P local took delivery of the cars and hauled them on to Black Butte, interchange point with Southern Pacific.

Overall, the CO&P averaged 3,300 cars a month in the first four months of 1997 — considerably higher than the levels for the first four months in 1996. According to Walt Brickwedel, CO&P's assistant to the general manager, traffic was up in part because of a new raw log move

"NEW LOOK"
Burlington Northern Santa Fe Railway
DASH 9-44CWs #1070 and #1069
Fallbridge Subdivision
Columbia River Gorge
November 20, 1996
Photo by Chris Jaques

between a Roseburg Forest Products facility in Weed, California, and another RFP mill in Dillard, Oregon. "The rest of the increase is just from getting more business from existing customers," Brickwedel explained. He added that carloadings of lumber and panel products, including plywood and particleboard, were headed up.

The fledgling carrier hauled a total of 40,000 cars in 1996, according to Central Oregon & Pacific general manager Bob Libby.

Brickwedel offered an example of how much the region's shortlines have come to depend on each other for business. He pointed out that Coos Bay District connection partner Longview, Portland & Northern — which has gone through a number of temporary shutdowns in recent years — was vital to the CO&P's health.

"The LP&N ships approximately 300 cars a month," Brickwedel said. "When they go down, we lose 10 percent of our carloadings, so that hurts."

Elsewhere, Washington's Tacoma Eastern Railway, based in Tacoma, signed a long-term lease to handle operations on 124 miles of three former Milwaukee Road lines in western Washington. Much of the trackage had been operated previously by the Weyerhaeuser-owned Chehalis Western Railroad.

"It's like opening a store and hoping the customers will come," said Dave Sprau, superintendent of the Tacoma Eastern.

On August 18, 1995, Oregon's Portland & Western Railroad fired up its engines on 63.4 miles of what had been Southern Pacific branchlines, primarily south and west of Portland. The carrier leased a portion of SP's Tillamook Branch (from Schefflin to Willsburg Junction); a segment of the West Side Branch (Cook to Newberg); and what SP had referred to as its West Side-Seghers Branch (from Hillsboro to the Stimson Timber mill near Seghers). Then, on September 1, 1995, the Portland & Western added three more lines, all previously operated by BN: the Forest Grove Branch (BN Junction to Forest Grove); a portion of the Oregon Electric Branch (Greton to Quinaby), and the remainder of the Vernonia Branch (Banks-Bendemeer). And on July 12, 1997, the P&W added the former BNSF Astoria Line between Willbridge and Astoria — approximately 95 miles — to its operating territory.

Despite all the transactions, a number of lines owned by the large carriers were simply torn up. One of the earliest routes to go in the contemporary reappraisal of branchline operations in the Northwest was SP's Wilkins Branch between Springfield and Tallman in Oregon, which was abandoned in December 1985.

In 1993, BN removed the 42-mile Goldendale Branch between Lyle

"GATEWAY"
Burlington Northern Santa Fe Railway
GP39-2 #2709/GP39 #2756/GP39 #2907
Oregon Trunk Subdivision
Bieber, California
May 1996

and Goldendale, Washington. Another loss was BN's short branch between Salem and West Salem, Oregon, which crossed the Willamette River. This connection was severed in 1996.

BN also eliminated its 42-mile Pendleton Branch, which ran south from Wallula, Washington, to Pendleton via Smeltz, Oregon. Service on the line was abandoned in 1991.

Union Pacific pulled up the rails and ties on two of its Washington branches — Colfax to Fairfield and Thornton to Seltice — in 1992.

In eastern Oregon, UP sold its 157-mile Oregon Eastern Branch, between Ontario and Burns, in November 1989. The purchaser was the Wyoming/Colorado Railroad, based in Laramie, Wyoming. After less than three years of marginal service, however, the shortline scrapped most of the line, leaving only 23 miles (from Ontario to Celatom) of the former UP route. The move upset state transportation officials, who had fought to have the line — severely damaged during flooding in Oregon's Harney Basin in 1984 — rebuilt with federal funds in 1990.

UP also lopped off most of the southern reaches of its Condon Branch in Oregon, where less than 12 miles — between Arlington and Gilliam — of what was once a 44-mile line remain in use. The rest of the branch that went south to Condon (and once connected with the previously-abandoned 24-mile shortline Condon, Kinzua & Southern), came up in 1993 after abandonment proceedings. The only thing that kept the last portion of the once-busy agricultural route from blowing away like the tumbleweeds that roll through this dry region was other people's trash: UP serves a 2,000-acre landfill at MP 11.5 with garbage trains that haul waste from Portland and Seattle five days a week.

Two Oregon shortlines owned by lumber companies were transformed into hiking trails in the mid-1990s. The Oregon, Pacific & Eastern Railway, which ended rail operations on November 22, 1993, ended up as a hiking trail after 14 miles of the line were torn out in 1994. To salvage at least some of the history of the route, the Bureau of Land Management moved quickly to set up a trail — called the "Row River Trail" — on the former Bohemia Corporation line, which had been used to serve Bohemia's lumber mills at Culp Creek.

Also being reduced to a hiking and biking trail was the Oregon, California & Eastern Railway, a 65-mile Weyerhaeuser logging railroad

"WHO MERGED WHO?"
Union Pacific Railroad
SP SD70M #9808
SP SD60 #9766
SP SD70M #9810
Portland Subdivision
Columbia River Gorge
January 15, 1997

between Klamath Falls and Bly in southern Oregon. The last log train snaked its way from Bly to Klamath Falls on April 29, 1990, and in 1995, the route became known as the "OC&E Rails-to-Trails Linear State Park."

In Washington, the 8-mile former Union Pacific branch from Pullman to Moscow — purchased by the Palouse River Railroad in November 1992 — was taken out of service after a 1996 flood damaged bridges and washed out long sections of track. Rather than repair and reopen the line, it instead was eventually turned into a paved hiking trail called the "Bill Chipman Palouse Trail." Fortunately for shippers in Moscow, where the tracks now come to an end, the paralleling Burlington Northern line remained operable, allowing for continued rail service between Pullman and Moscow. The line is now operated by the Palouse River & Coulee City Railroad.

Economic realities doomed some Northwest lines. A route that couldn't be saved was the 1.9-mile Mountain Fir Branch of the Willamette Valley Railroad. It quit operations on the line from Independence to Mountain Fir, Oregon, when the only shipper on the trackage — a Mountain Fir Lumber Company mill — closed in 1992. The route, which ran from a connection with SP at V&S Junction to a lumber mill at Mountain Fir, was taken out of service after the mill went out of business. The tracks were removed in 1995. Thus, the final significant remnant of what had once been the 41-mile Valley & Siletz Railroad was lost.

Also in 1995, the Willamina & Grand Ronde Railway, which was under the same ownership as the Willamette Valley Railroad, sold its 5.2-mile route between Willamina and Fort Hill, Oregon. The buyer was Hampton Railway, the company that operates the lumber mill at the end of the line in Fort Hill. After the deal was struck, Hampton Railway contracted with the Willamette & Pacific to provide switching service as needed to its mill.

As the Willamette Valley Railroad contracted on one side of the Willamette Valley, however, it was expanding on the other. In 1993 it

"NOW YOU SEE IT"
Southern Pacific Railroad
Modoc Line
Alturas, California
May 24, 1996

Taking the big curve at the Alturas, California, wye, a 45-car Southern Pacific mixed merchandise train heads north on the threatened Modoc Line at noon on May 24, 1996. Powering the train are SP locomotives SD45T-2 #9345, SD45T-2 #9391, and SD40T-2 #6838. The woodchip cars in the background are waiting to be hauled to Lakeview, Oregon, by the shortline Great Western Railway, which bought the former SP Lakeview Branch in 1986. The SP freight is running on the "now you see it, now you don't" Modoc Line through route between Flanigan, Nevada, and Klamath Falls, Oregon. SP mothballed the line in the late 1980s, but when Denver & Rio Grande Western purchased SP in 1988, the route — nearly 250 miles shorter than the Shasta Line for traffic bound from Oregon to the Midwest — was reopened to line-haul operations. Union Pacific, which merged SP into its system in September 1996, plans to abandon the line between Alturas and Wendel, California, approximately 100 miles.

leased the former SP West Stayton Branch between Woodburn and Stayton, Oregon (31 miles); the ex-SP Mill City Branch between Albany and Mill City, Oregon (48 miles); and the ex-SP Geer Branch from Salem to Geer, Oregon, another seven miles. The Geer Branch didn't last long, however: most of it was abandoned in late 1995.

The Molalla Western, which operated on the former SP 10.4-mile Molalla Branch from Canby to Molalla, Oregon, finally pulled back from the rarely-used southern end of its line in 1996. The last quarter-mile of track into Molalla, which had been out of service for several months prior to the decision to cut it off, was abandoned and removed near the end of that year.

As part of the process, the three-track switching yard at Molalla and the signal lights protecting the grade crossing on Oregon Highway 211 through the city were removed. Thus, rails were suddenly absent from Molalla for the first time since the railroad — in its inception as an electric interurban route — first reached the town in 1912.

North of Molalla, the tracks are being used for storage of surplus freight cars, as well as brand new cars from freight car builder Gunderson. In 1996, dozens of new Southern Pacific boxcars — reported to be the last freight car order SP placed before it was merged with UP — and bright-yellow DTTX container flats were waiting among the meadow flowers for a call to service.

"STOP HERE"
Amtrak's *Pioneer*
Pendleton, Oregon
April 23, 1997

Pausing in Pendleton, Oregon, crew members of the Amtrak Pioneer grab a standing cup of coffee and share a laugh before boarding F40PH #400 and heading eastward to Chicago via La Grande, Boise, and Salt Lake City. The "Amtrak Stop Here" sign is ironic: within less than three weeks, the route would be axed by Amtrak.

Dick Samuels, owner of the Molalla Western and the East Portland Traction Company, decided to cover them under the same name to "avoid having to do two sets of paperwork," he explained. On January 1, 1997, Samuels' combined roads became known as the Oregon Pacific Railroad Company.

The Port of Tillamook Bay Railroad (POTB) suffered severe damage in a February 1996 flood, as water and mudslides washed away sections of the roadbed. About seven miles of track, trestles and tunnels in the Salmonberry River Canyon were damaged heavily, especially between Enright and Cochran, Oregon. However, with financial assistance from the Federal Emergency Management Agency, the line was eventually returned to service.

However, in a situation that appears to be becoming more prevalent in recent years, some people jumped on the cost of repairing the flood damage to push for abandonment of the POTB's 90-mile railroad line between Tillamook and Hillsboro. Some hotel owners in Rockaway Beach, for example, contended that the movement of trains hurt the local economy. Rockaway Beach City Council member Toni Hatfield, who owns a motel in the coastal town, suggested that the line should be abandoned to eliminate "interference" from trains that briefly halt traffic — a few times a week — and shake buildings.

The 21-mile Mount Hood Railroad, based in Hood River, Oregon, was having troubles as well. The carrier lost a good customer when the Dee Forest Products hardboard plant at Dee burned down on November 16, 1996. As a result, the southernmost 13 miles of the former UP branchline route sees no more freight traffic, although passenger trains ply the rails from Hood River to Parkdale much of the year. The shortline's biggest remaining customer is a propane gas shipper at Pine Grove. Due to the declines in business, the Mount Hood Railroad was trying to maintain scheduled freight runs on Wednesday and Friday, "but some weeks we don't even do that. It's the slowest it's ever been," said one employee. "We had six fruit cars last year. I remember when we had 100 to 150 cars a year."

To make things worse, the Mount Hood Railroad was hit hard by the flooding in February 1996, and suffered close to $500,000 worth of damage. More than 1,000 feet of track washed out near Powerdale, and culverts along the line were destroyed. The line was completely out of service for two months.

Meanwhile, Washington Central Railroad's branchlines in the Yakima Valley — which WCRC had obtained from Burlington Northern in October 1986 — reverted to BNSF control with the 1996 merger of the two carriers. Not surprisingly, BNSF did not want to take over any new feeder branch operations after years of shedding routes. So the lines between Moses Lake and Connell, Washington, were leased to the Columbia Basin Railroad.

Another new Washington shortline was the 21-mile Toppenish, Simcoe & Western, formed in 1993 to serve a former Washington Central branch. The TS&W operates from a connection with BNSF at Toppenish to White Swan, Washington.

In June 1997, co-owners BNSF and UP announced their intent to sell the 245-mile Camas Prairie Railroad, based in Lewiston, Idaho. Ownership of the shortline was mixed because predecessor roads of both large carriers built routes that later became part of the Camas Prairie. In 1997, the Camas Prairie maintained service on four different routes: Lewiston to Kooskia, Idaho, 74.5 miles; Riparia, Washington, to East Lewiston, Idaho, 70.5 miles; Spalding to Grangeville, Idaho, 66.5 miles; and Revling to Orofino, Idaho, 31.0 miles.

Farther to the west, two of BNSF's busiest Northwest feeders were located in the sparsely populated areas of Washington's Olympic Peninsula: the 56.2-mile Harbor Line Subdivision, which runs west from Centralia to Aberdeen and Hoquiam; and the 67.4-mile Bangor Subdivision, which connects Elma and Bangor. Despite the volume of traffic on the branchlines (trains operate six days a week from Centralia to Shelton, and five days a week from Elma to Bangor and Hoquiam), BNSF put out the word in May 1997 that these lines, too, were going up for sale. It wasn't long before a buyer was found. On August 30, 1997,

a new carrier — the Puget Sound & Pacific Railroad — started operations on the former Northern Pacific property. The railroad's chairman, Dave Parkinson, also runs the Arizona & California Railroad and the California Northern Railroad.

Truly, there appeared to be little patience for nurturing the branchline feeders that once penetrated into virtually every backwater crossroads in the Northwest's rural heartland. Instead, the big railroads were streamlining to their core line-haul routes.

And another subtle yet significant development was taking place in the mid-1990s. Whereas previously it had been the rail lines themselves that were in danger of disappearing, all at once it seemed to be the familiar paint schemes and corporate identities that were fading fast. An avalanche of changes was hitting the industry; changes that would have a huge impact on railroad operations in the Pacific Northwest.

In October 1995, Union Pacific Railroad absorbed the Chicago & NorthWestern Railroad, a $1.2 billion takeover. In the months following the transaction, C&NW locomotives became a relatively common sight in the power mix of UP freights systemwide.

UP, however, didn't content itself with taking over the C&NW and its 5,800 miles of track. Always aggressive, UP moved rapidly — many contend too rapidly — to take over the 11,000-mile Southern Pacific Railroad as well.

On July 3, 1996, the Surface Transportation Board (STB) handed down its ruling on UP's bold bid. There had been strong protests from some quarters — including the U.S. Department of Agriculture, the U.S. Department of Transportation, and the anti-trust division of the Justice Department, along with neighboring railroads Conrail and Kansas City Southern — but the board sorted through UP's 15-volume, 8,100-page merger application and voted 3-0 to approve the transaction. It was a $5.4 billion deal that UP officials contended would save the railroad $750 million a year, while upgrading freight service in Western states. In fact, UP pledged to pump $1.3 billion worth of capital improvements into the former SP infrastructure between 1996 and 2000. (Ironically,

Looking south on Southern Pacific's West Side Branch, just outside of Corvallis, Oregon. The straight north-south line, which ends 17.3 miles away in Monroe, is used a couple times a week to access a handful of argicultural and wood products shippers south of the Willamette Valley college town. SP vacated the property in February 1993; the Willamette & Pacific Railroad now operates on the line.

"GO SOUTH"
Southern Pacific Railroad
West Side Branch
Corvallis, Oregon
February 1990

Santa Fe had tried to merge with SP in a $5.2 billion stock swap in 1983, a move the ICC shot down.)

The UP/SP merger became official on September 12, 1996, creating a new rail system with 35,800 miles of track.

The owners of two Oregon shortlines had differing views on the merger. Dick Samuels of the Oregon Pacific said he wasn't too happy about Union Pacific's takeover of Southern Pacific.

"It's really bad," Samuels complained. "I'm having trouble convincing them that getting 75 cars all at once is not the same as getting 25 cars a week. Any industry that gives them 1,500 cars a year would have a better agreement with UP, and better service."

David Root, co-owner of the Willamette Valley Railroad, said he was glad SP was taken over by UP.

"With UP, it's a whole changed picture," he said. "It's a lot easier working with them than the SP. It's helped a lot."

The final shape of UP's expansion, however, was not without some strings attached. The STB placed 35 conditions on UP before it granted its stamp of approval, including that UP would have to grant BNSF 4,000 miles worth of trackage rights across the new UP/SP network. In addition, UP and BNSF agreed on a transaction that would convey the UP's "Inside Gateway" (former Western Pacific) trackage between Bieber and Keddie, California, to BNSF.

The passage of SP could not be foreseen with any certainty as late as 1994, and what seemed almost too common in the early 1990s is now a part of history. How fast the landscape can change.

In a guest column in *The Oregonian* in August 1996, Dan Butler — a part-time engineer on the Willamette & Pacific Railroad — wrote a sensitive commentary on the demise of Southern Pacific. Butler captured the essence of what the merger meant to Oregon with these words:

"... Crossing both the Cascades and Siskiyous, with a main line running the length of the state and three routes to the coast — from Medford to Molalla, Oregon was SP territory. At one time, every backwater berg from Coquille to Corvallis, and places like Willamina, Silverton, and Drain, all connected via numerous branchlines to the massive SP system that stretched through California into the Southwest and east to St. Louis ..."

Butler hit it squarely. SP, perhaps more than any other carrier, symbolized Western railroading, and on an emotional level, its loss was unfortunate — especially when UP stated that the merger would result in the tearing up of much of SP's Modoc Line (the 220-mile route extended from Klamath Falls, Oregon, to Flanigan, Nevada, via Alturas, California). UP officials also said they anticipated a substantial downgrading of operations at SP's Eugene Yard — the largest SP facility in Oregon — in favor of expansion at UP's Albina Yard in Portland.

While all this was going on, Burlington Northern had certainly not been idle. Even before the UP/SP merger plans were announced, the

Interstate Commerce Commission had approved, in a 4-0 vote in 1995, a merger of Burlington Northern Inc. and Santa Fe Pacific Corporation, parent company of the Atchison, Topeka & Santa Fe Railway. The new system, efficiently referred to as BNSF, comprised 31,000 miles of track in 27 states and two Canadian provinces. The ICC's decision to shine a green light on the BN/Santa Fe merger became official on August 23, 1995, clearing the way for what was, briefly, the nation's largest railroad — until UP gobbled up C&NW and SP.

Thus, the quintessential image that symbolized the alterations in the Northwest's railroads, especially in the mid- to late-1990s, could be simplified to this: Locomotives were changing colors. UP's yellow units reached into new places, places where they'd rarely been welcome before. (In fact, some observers were referring to the UP expansion as the "yellow tide.") SP and C&NW paint schemes, on the other hand, were disappearing into the fog of history. Many of the scenes recorded in this book will never be repeated, and the fleeting presence of dozens of locomotives from C&NW and SP in traditional UP territory will likely become only a historical footnote.

The news concerning passenger train operations across the Northwest was a mixture of good and bad in the 1990s. For example, on May 26, 1995, Amtrak restored service between Seattle and Vancouver, British Columbia, for the first time in 14 years, as the *Mount Baker International* restarted daily operations along the route. But the thrice-weekly *Pioneer* — which rolled between Chicago and Seattle via Denver, La Grande, The Dalles, Hood River, and Portland — was endangered to the point of extinction: the train did not survive 1997.

"We looked at which trains could perform more effectively in terms of current ridership and what was projected," said Amtrak spokesperson Dominick Albano in Oakland, California. "We think there will be an increase on *The Empire Builder*. It's held steady near 50 percent, and we expect it to be up to 75 percent occupancy in the future. *The Pioneer,* on the other hand, averaged only 35 percent occupancy."

Excursion carriers encountered trouble as well. Among the casualties was the *Spirit of Oregon,* a classy dinner train operating on the former SP Tillamook Branch in the foothills of Oregon's Coast Range. It terminated operations in August 1996. However, the train itself resurfaced eight months later in Hood River, when the Mount Hood Railroad leased the entire *Spirit of Oregon* trainset on a one-year trial basis.

In Washington, the *Spirit of Washington* dinner train left Yakima in May 1992 and moved its operations to Renton, where it leases BNSF's former Northern Pacific line between Renton and Woodinville, 23 miles. Operators said there were not enough customers to support it on its previous runs between Yakima and Ellensburg.

The basic concept of *Rolling Dreams: Portraits of the Northwest's Railroad Heritage* is to get away from the urban centers and focus primarily on railroads traversing rural environs. Geographically, *Rolling Dreams* stretches out to cover an area that ranges across Oregon and Washington as well as glancing into northern California. In this endeavor, I hope to preserve a small piece of the Northwest's railroad environment, and visually celebrate the region's rail heritage in the waning years of the 20th century.

By no means does this book strive to feature photos of every scenic station, every colorful locomotive, and every pristine rail corridor across the great Northwest. Rather it is designed to provide a cross-section of definitive images in a period stretching from the late 1980s to the late 1990s.

The motivation behind *Rolling Dreams* is to offer a photographic sketch of railroad settings during a time of rapid realignments in the overall rail network of the West. The purpose is to visualize some of the key details of what has transpired in the past several years, but more than that, to capture the feeling of what it has meant to witness the sudden transition.

Rolling Dreams is dedicated to the spirit of the Northwest's unfolding railroad tales: boxcars rolling through the star-filled night; moonlight shining off the sides of swaying cars; the sweet scent of woodchips and creosote pulled along in the breezy wake of a passing freight; the faint note of a distant locomotive's air horn reaching back across the open land.

— *D. C. Jesse Burkhardt*
White Salmon, Washington
September 1, 1997

"MERGER LINEUP"
Union Pacific Railroad
C&NW SD60 #8730/SP SD45T-2 #9343/UP SD60M #6165
The Dalles, Oregon
December 1996

❝ *By and by they blew the highball whistle after the eastbound freight had smashed through on the mainline and we pulled out as the air got colder and fog began to blow from the sea over the warm valleys of the coast.* ❞

— Jack Kerouac, *"The Dharma Bums,"* 1959

I. On the Mainline: Tracks Through the Columbia River Gorge

There are two mainline routes that parallel each other on opposite sides of the magnificent Columbia River, which originates on the west slope of the Rocky Mountains in British Columbia and flows for 1,214 miles. The lines are Union Pacific's Portland Subdivision in Oregon and Spokane Subdivision in Washington, and Burlington Northern Santa Fe's Fallbridge Subdivision and Wishram Subdivision in Washington.

Trains on these key lines, which pass through a portion of the Columbia Gorge National Scenic Area, provide a representative cross-section of the operations of the Northwest's new mega-carriers. These images allow a glimpse at operations before and during the mid-1990s, when Burlington Northern and Santa Fe joined forces and UP took control of two large interstate carriers: first Chicago & NorthWestern, and soon thereafter Southern Pacific.

In the Northwest, the yellow of Union Pacific locomotives became ever more common on the mainlines. For a magical couple of years, however, the colors of SP, C&NW, and UP mixed commonly, while across the river on Burlington Northern Santa Fe, Santa Fe paint schemes blended with Burlington Northern green and an assortment of leased power to provide a hint of mystery. When headlights appeared in the distance, there could never be any certainty as to what manner of locomotive would be doing the hauling.

In the late 1990s, as many as 30 or 40 trains a day race on opposite sides of the wide Columbia River, and that number is growing.

The competition appears to be fierce ...

A westbound autoracks train rocks through Lyle, Washington, with Burlington Northern SD40-2 #7185 on the point. Note the well-maintained trackage, including concrete ties.
"To effectively run a railroad and best serve customers requires investing in a top-notch physical plant," said Gus Melonas, BNSF's director of communications in Seattle. "A strong railroad begins with good trackage."

"AUTOS WEST"
Burlington Northern Santa Fe Railway
Fallbridge Subdivision
Lyle, Washington
June 1, 1996

"WESTBOUND TRIO"
Burlington Northern Railroad
Wishram Subdivision
Wishram, Washington
February 18, 1995

Three westbounds are lined up and waiting, a relatively unusual sight in Wishram in recent times. Since BN suspended crew changes at Wishram on November 1, 1994, the yard is seldom crowded. Indeed, in the mid-1990s, more often than not, the yard is virtually bare. Wishram had served as a crew-change point for trains traveling between Pasco and Vancouver for 83 years.

Even before the October 1995 absorption of Chicago & NorthWestern by Union Pacific, C&NW locomotives were occasionally seen in the Northwest. In March 1995, for instance, UP SD60M #6302 leads two C&NW SD60s (#8033 and #8054) hauling a long soda ash train through sleepy Mosier, Oregon, alongside the Columbia River.

"EARLY CLUE"
Union Pacific Railroad
Portland Subdivision
Mosier, Oregon
March 9, 1995

"LAST CALL"
Amtrak
The Pioneer
Rowena, Oregon
May 10, 1997

Amtrak's Pioneer *passenger train makes its final run west through the Columbia River Gorge with five passenger cars and a baggage car. The train, pictured here a couple miles west of Rowena, Oregon, is on its way to Portland and north from there to Seattle. The timing of the final train proved auspicious: In the background, a tug pushes a barge-load of containers along the Columbia River, while on the northern bank, a freight train rolls westward on Burlington Northern Santa Fe's Fallbridge Subdivision.*

"C&NW SIDING"
Union Pacific Railroad
Portland Subdivision
Wyeth, Oregon
February 24, 1996

Pulled by Chicago & NorthWestern SD40-2 #6903 and Union Pacific SD40-2 #3822, a westbound freight takes the siding at Wyeth, Oregon, on February 24, 1996, where it will wait briefly for an eastbound intermodal train. Almost immediately following Union Pacific's control of the Chicago & NorthWestern Railway on October 1, 1995, C&NW locomotives appeared with increasing frequency all across the UP system. By the end of 1996, however, UP's aggressive repainting program was making C&NW paint increasingly uncommon.

"MIRROR IMAGE"
Union Pacific Railroad
SD60M #6260/SD60M #6284/SD50 #5007/SD40-2 #3914
Portland Subdivision
Wyeth, Oregon
August 10, 1996

With windsurfers on the Columbia River in the background, a Burlington Northern Santa Fe freight — pulled by BN SD40-2 #7016, BN SD40-2 #7928, and Santa Fe SDP40F #5250 — heads north on the Oregon Trunk Branch at O.T. Junction, Oregon. Across the river is the train's destination: the freight yard at Wishram, Washington.

"O.T. JUNCTION"
Burlington Northern Santa Fe Railway
Oregon Trunk Subdivision
O.T. Junction, Oregon
August 1996

"DRAWBRIDGE"
Burlington Northern Railroad
Oregon Trunk Subdivision
O.T. Junction, Oregon
November 1995

Burlington Northern's Oregon Trunk Branch starts where it cuts away from the Columbia Gorge mainline at Wishram, Washington. The line runs south across the Columbia River, crossing the drawbridge to O.T. Junction, Oregon. In November 1995, a southbound train is coming over the river on its way toward Klamath Falls. Three BN "whiteface" units — all GP40s — pull the long train into Oregon; trailing in the distance, still in Washington, are two BN cabooses: #10024 and #12287.

"TRUCKIN'..."
Union Pacific Railroad
UP #25832
The Dalles, Oregon
August 1996

Union Pacific caboose #25832 rests in the freight yard at The Dalles, Oregon. Six days a week, UP puts a caboose on its local train operating out of The Dalles to Bend, Oregon, by way of trackage rights on Burlington Northern Santa Fe's Oregon Trunk Line. The logo on the cab's side recalls a time when railroads seemed to be more aggressive in their marketing efforts: "Keep on truckin'... by train."

"CONVERGENCE"
Union Pacific Railroad
Portland Subdivision
The Dalles, Oregon
March 5, 1997

A variety of locomotive types, colors, and road names briefly assemble near the Union Pacific station in The Dalles, Oregon, on March 5, 1997. Included in the colorful scene are Southern Pacific SD45T-2 #7430, in the infamous, aborted "merger" (with Santa Fe) paint scheme, and Denver & Rio Grande Western GP40-2 #3109. Also on hand are UP GP38-2s #2040, #2053, and #2037, along with UP SD60 #6238.

27

"EASTBOUND EMPTIES"
Burlington Northern Santa Fe Railway
Fallbridge Subdivision
East Bingen, Washington
April 12, 1997

With desert parsley blooming, a Burlington Northern Santa Fe "grain empties" train pulls out of the siding at East Bingen, Washington, rolling eastbound alongside the Columbia River. The long freight is headed by two units in BNSF's new paint scheme.

"ON THE RIVER"
Union Pacific Railroad
Portland Subdivision
Columbia River Gorge
February 16, 1997

"THE RACE"
Burlington Northern Railroad
Fallbridge Subdivision
Columbia River Gorge
April 14, 1996

A Burlington Northern eastbound freight "races" a paralleling speedboat on the Columbia River, the green locomotives blending in as if camouflaged against the rich spring grass on the bluffs. A grab-bag of four different BN units — GP39-2 #2707, GP40-2 #3054, B30-7AB #4020 (cabless), and SD40-2 #7905 — power the train, which is on its way to Pasco, Washington.

"TREASURE IN TRASH"
Burlington Northern Santa Fe Railway
Wishram Subdivision
West Maryhill, Washington
October 26, 1996

A garbage-hauling train passes through West Maryhill as it returns from the Rabanco Regional Disposal Company landfill at Roosevelt, Washington, with empty containers. The containers are on their way back to Seattle, where they will quickly be refilled and then sent back to Roosevelt, a small village in eastern Klickitat County. Garbage from the Seattle area, as well as from California's Napa Valley and from Alaska, is being transported to Roosevelt in an endless cycle, creating a steady business that is increasingly lucrative for the railroad. The landfill at Roosevelt takes in approximately 200,000 tons of trash a month.

"GP50 EAST"
Burlington Northern Santa Fe Railway
Fallbridge Subdivision
North Dalles, Washington
July 1997

"SNOW TOWERS"
Southern Pacific Railroad
Tillamook Branch
Cook, Oregon
February 1989

❝ *The train went on up the track out of sight, around one of the hills of burnt timber . . . There was no town, nothing but the rails and the burned over country.* ❞

— Ernest Hemingway, *"Big Two-Hearted River,"* 1925

II. Nothing but the Rails: Branchlines and Shortlines

The lines are often poorly maintained. The rail is light and worn, the ties splintering. Ballast, sometimes, is almost non-existent; as if the tracks and ties had been placed right on the ground with little preparation of the right-of-way.

Traffic on the Northwest's feeder routes has survived into the late 1990s. Yet with serious economic problems facing rural communities and their shippers, it is questionable whether these lines will endure much longer.

At least for now, however, local trains continue to rock faithfully along on a network of backwater routes, hauling a variety of cargo behind a multi-colored diversity of motive power ...

33

"DALLAS BRANCH"
Southern Pacific Railroad
Dallas, Oregon
October 5, 1990

Southern Pacific's Corvallis-based Dallas Local rolls west toward Dallas, Oregon. The train, operating on Mondays, Wednesdays, and Fridays, serves three primary customers: a Willamette Industries sawmill in Dallas, agricultural shippers at Derry, and the Willamette Valley Railroad interchange at V&S Junction. On this day's run, SP SD9 #4402 pulls seven empty boxcars and an out-of-place caboose alongside a bit of rural Oregon's pristine scenery, just before a strong rain soaks the area.

"WILD MUSTARD"
Southern Pacific Railroad
SD9 #4363
Dallas Branch
Dallas, Oregon
March 27, 1991

Southern Pacific SD9 #4363 parades its bright colors across rural ranchlands as it ambles west toward Dallas, Oregon, on the 5.3-mile Dallas Branch. The wild mustard flowers blooming all around the train closely match the locomotive's colors, yet the paint scheme was almost as fleeting as the springtime flowers: When Southern Pacific and Santa Fe officials discussed merger in the early 1980s, the two railroad companies were so convinced their plan would eventually be approved by the Interstate Commerce Commission that they gave many of their locomotives a new paint job in anticipation of the partnership. Note how the configuration leaves room to add a big "SF" next to the SP letters. Unfortunately for the railroads, however, the merger application was rejected by the ICC in July 1986, and overnight, units in the red and yellow colors this one displays became something of an embarrassment to executives of the two railroads. Indeed, some creative thinker came up with a clever twist on the would-be "SPSF" acronym: "Shouldn't Paint So Fast."

"OUTBOUND LOADS"
Southern Pacific Railroad
Bailey Branch
Bailey, Oregon
July 17, 1990

"COUNTY CROSSING"
Southern Pacific Railroad
West Side Branch
Greenberry, Oregon
November 1, 1990

Rural Oregon, 1990: County road meets railroad crossing, as Southern Pacific's twice-weekly Dawson Local cuts southbound, splitting through the crossbucks with the rain-swept Coast Range Mountains towering in the background. In the early 1990s, SD9s were still an everyday sight, as they were standard power on SP branches. In this November scene, SP SD9 #4410 pulls a short train toward a backwoods lumber mill.

"HELPERS"
Central Oregon & Pacific Railroad
Siskiyou District
Siskiyou Summit, Oregon
May 29, 1996

The Central Oregon & Pacific, a newcomer to Oregon, took over two former Southern Pacific branches (the Coos Bay Line and the Siskiyou Line) on December 31, 1994. Six months later — on June 5, 1995 — CO&P reopened SP's dormant crossing of the Siskiyou Mountains, which SP had embargoed in August 1992 due to declining carloads. CO&P normally employs helper sets on its through operations across the Siskiyou Range. In this scene from May 1996, a CO&P brakeman swings closed a switch after cutting out three freshly-washed helpers — GP38s #5532, #5057, and #5047 — from the rear of the day's southbound Montague Hauler. At Montague, California, approximately 37 miles to the south, cars coming over the line are handed off to the crew of the Weed Local, a CO&P train based in Weed, California. The local will ferry them to the Union Pacific interchange at Black Butte, where the Shasta Line and Siskiyou Line meet.

"OUT OF SERVICE"
Burlington Northern Railroad (ex-SP&S Railway)
Vernonia Branch
Banks, Oregon
July 1990

"SWITCHSTAND"
Burlington Northern Railroad
Forest Grove Branch
Forest Grove, Oregon
July 25, 1990

Leased GP38-2 #771 comes around a corner at Forest Grove, Oregon, with a short string of cars for the Gray & Company cherry packing plant at the end of Burlington Northern's Forest Grove Branch. The old switchstand and shaky condition of the rails and roadbed tells much about the line's uncertain future. In the early 1990s, BN served customers along the 5.7-mile route on Mondays, Wednesdays, and Fridays, with a local train based in Beaverton. In September 1995, new shortline Portland & Western Railroad took over service on the branch.

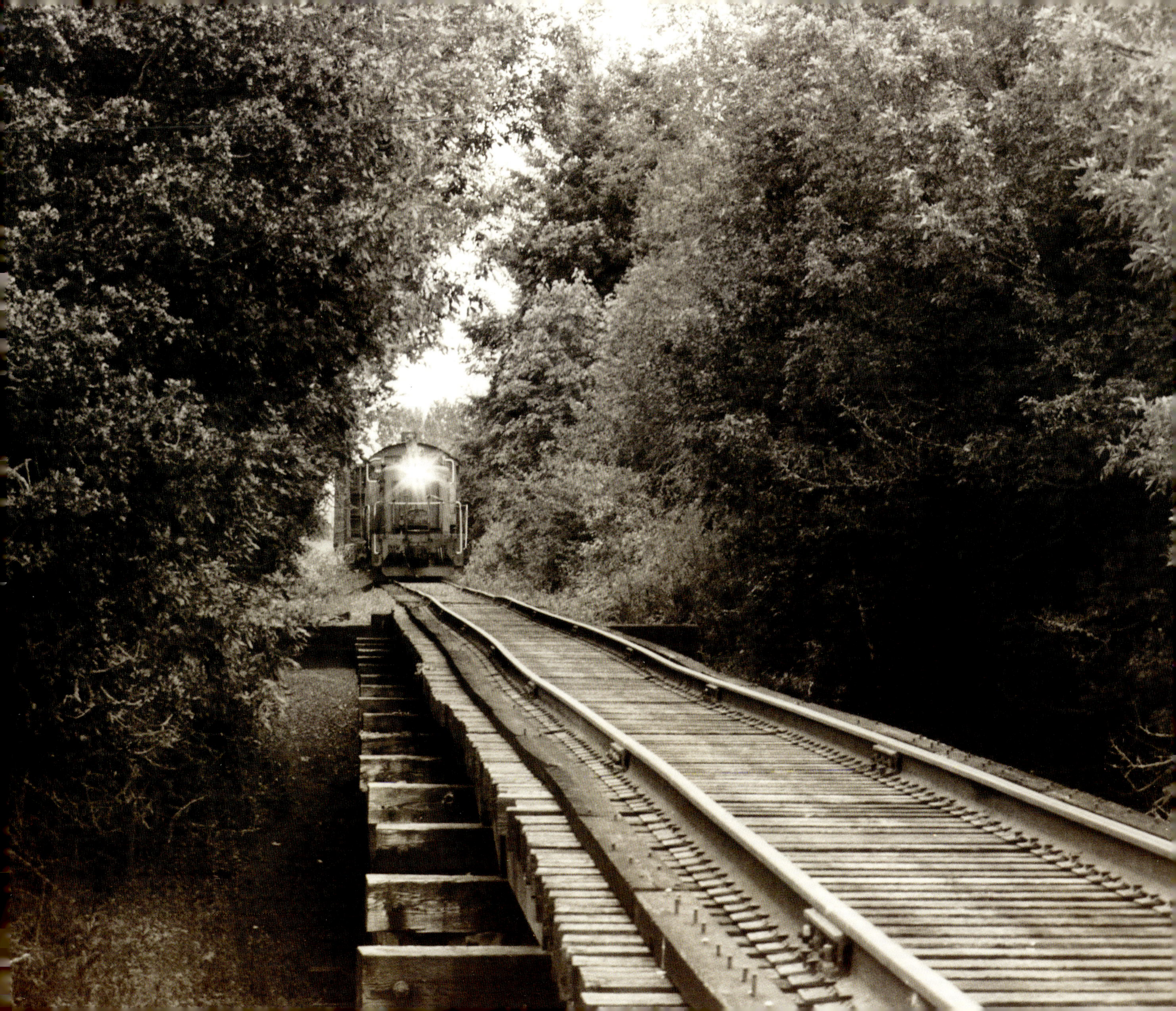

◀ **"REMNANT"**
Willamette Valley Railroad
Mountain Fir, Oregon
June 1991

Just west of Independence, Oregon, half of the Willamette Valley Railroad's locomotive roster — ex-SP SW1200 #2274 — is hauling several empty flatcars toward the line's sole shipper, Mountain Fir Lumber Company. The train is traveling along two miles of wavy track that is a remnant of the 41-mile Valley & Siletz Railroad, most of which was abandoned in the mid-1980s. The mill at the end of the line closed in 1992; the tracks were removed two years later.

"BETTER DAYS"
Willamette Valley Railroad
WVRD GP9 #2890
Independence, Oregon
April 1995

At the Willamette Valley Railroad's headquarters in Independence, Oregon, in April 1995, ex-Southern Pacific GP9 #2890 — built by EMD in 1959 — rusts away in the elements, long out of service.

"SNOW COVER"
City of Prineville Railway
COP #7139
Hood River, Oregon
January 1996

"CATTAIL TRESTLE"
Southern Pacific Railroad
SD9 #4326
West Side-Seghers Branch
Carnation, Oregon
September 21, 1990

Southern Pacific's Seghers Local heads south along the West Side-Seghers Branch. As the weekend approaches, SP SD9 #4326 is on its way to pick up two boxcar loads at the Stimson Timber mill in Seghers, 12 miles south of Hillsboro.

"BN LOGGER"
Burlington Northern Railroad
Santiam Branch
Foster, Oregon
March 27, 1991

"ECLECTIC MIX"
Burlington Northern Railroad
GP38-2 #780/SW1500 #321
Oregon Electric Branch
Cartney, Oregon
June 26, 1991

Leased GP38-2 #780 and Burlington Northern SW1500 #321 pull boxcars loaded with grass seed out of the spur track at Cartney, Oregon, on Burlington Northern's Oregon Electric Branch. A tremendous volume of seed is hauled along this route, with summer bringing a massive increase in tonnage moving off the line. More than 90% of all grass seed produced in the United States comes from the Willamette Valley of Oregon, and Burlington Northern shares in the annual bounty.
Note the large "O" and "E" on the top corners of the moss-covered concrete building behind the locomotives. The structure, now used as a seed warehouse, is a former Oregon Electric passenger depot, a stark reminder of the line's interurban origins.

"FOR THE HAULER"
Longview, Portland & Northern Railway
Gardiner Junction, Oregon
July 23, 1993

The engineer of Longview, Portland & Northern's Alco S2 switcher #111, "Thomas Kopriva," looks over his switching list while dropping off a cut of boxcars at Gardiner Junction, Oregon, in July 1993. The boxcars, from the International Paper Company mill in nearby Gardiner, will be left on a siding adjacent to Southern Pacific's Coos Bay Branch, which runs between Eugene and Coquille. The freight cars will be picked up later in the day by SP's Eugene-bound Coos Bay Hauler.

"JUNCTION"
Southern Pacific Railroad
Willamina Local
Whiteson, Oregon
July 20, 1990

On an overcast Friday, Southern Pacific's Willamina Local, behind SD9s #4302 and #4408, arrives at a junction in Whiteson, Oregon, where the West Side Branch and the 18.7-mile Willamina Branch converge. From here, the train will fork off to the west to serve branchline shippers and interchange cars with the Willamina & Grand Ronde Railway at Willamina. SP operated this train five days a week out of McMinnville, until leasing the line to the Willamette & Pacific Railroad in 1993. Two SD9s were standard power on the run.

"THE PAINT KEEPS CHANGING"
Bailey Branch
Dawson, Oregon

The Hull-Oakes Lumber Company in Dawson, Oregon, sits at the end of a 6.9-mile line known as the Bailey Branch, and it provides enough loads of lumber to keep the trains coming. In these three views that span an eight-year period, three different paint schemes are seen, and each one tells a story ...

In the top photo, Southern Pacific SD9 #4431 is working the mill in February 1988. Note the stacked package of headlights. Until the early 1990s, most SP units had a similar light package, which featured oscillating headlights as a safety feature. In the center photo, taken in March 1991, the oscillating lights are gone, and the paint scheme reflects a merger plan that failed. SP and Santa Fe were ready to combine operations, and jointly came up with a fresh corporate image, hence the new paint. But in something of a surprise at the time, the Interstate Commerce Commission voted to deny the transaction. After the deal fell through, these units often ended up being given low-profile assignments. SP SD9 #4363 saw a lot of service on western Oregon branchlines in the months after the merger proposal collapsed ...

Southern Pacific Railroad
SP SD9 #4431
February 16, 1988

Southern Pacific Railroad
SP SD9 #4363
March 19, 1991

By 1993, SP had exited from the branchline. A new regional carrier, the Willamette & Pacific Railroad, took over operations on several former SP branches in Oregon, including the Bailey Branch. In this photo, Willamette & Pacific GP9 #1801, ex-SP #3855, is shown switching the Hull-Oakes sawmill on April 13, 1995. As if in tribute to the line's history, W&P chose the old Southern Pacific "Black Widow" paint scheme for this unit.

Willamette & Pacific Railroad
W&P GP9 #1801
April 13, 1995

"FORGOTTEN RAILS"
Burlington Northern Railroad
Astoria Line
Astoria, Oregon
July 1990

"RAINY DAY TRAINS"
Mount Hood Railroad
Hood River, Oregon
August 1995

During a hard rain in August 1995, Mount Hood GP9 #88, pulling two bulkhead flatcars of lumber, passes Amtrak's westbound **Pioneer** *in front of the combined Mount Hood Railroad/Amtrak depot in Hood River, Oregon.*

"WAIT IN THE WEEDS"
Port of Tillamook Bay Railroad
SD9 #4361
Banks, Oregon
June 14, 1989

On a rainy February day, three of the Port of Tillamook Bay Railroad's six ex-SP SD9s — #4381, #4368, and #4406, each in a different paint scheme — pause at the Banks Lumber Company mill in Banks, Oregon, before hauling a string of empties over the Coast Range to Tillamook.

"SD9 PAINT"
Port of Tillamook Bay Railroad
Banks, Oregon
February 1, 1997

"SEMAPHORE FRAME"
Southern Pacific Railroad
Siskiyou Line
Drain, Oregon
July 23, 1993

A northbound Southern Pacific freight, framed by a trestle over Pass Creek, rolls toward semaphore towers on the Siskiyou Line.

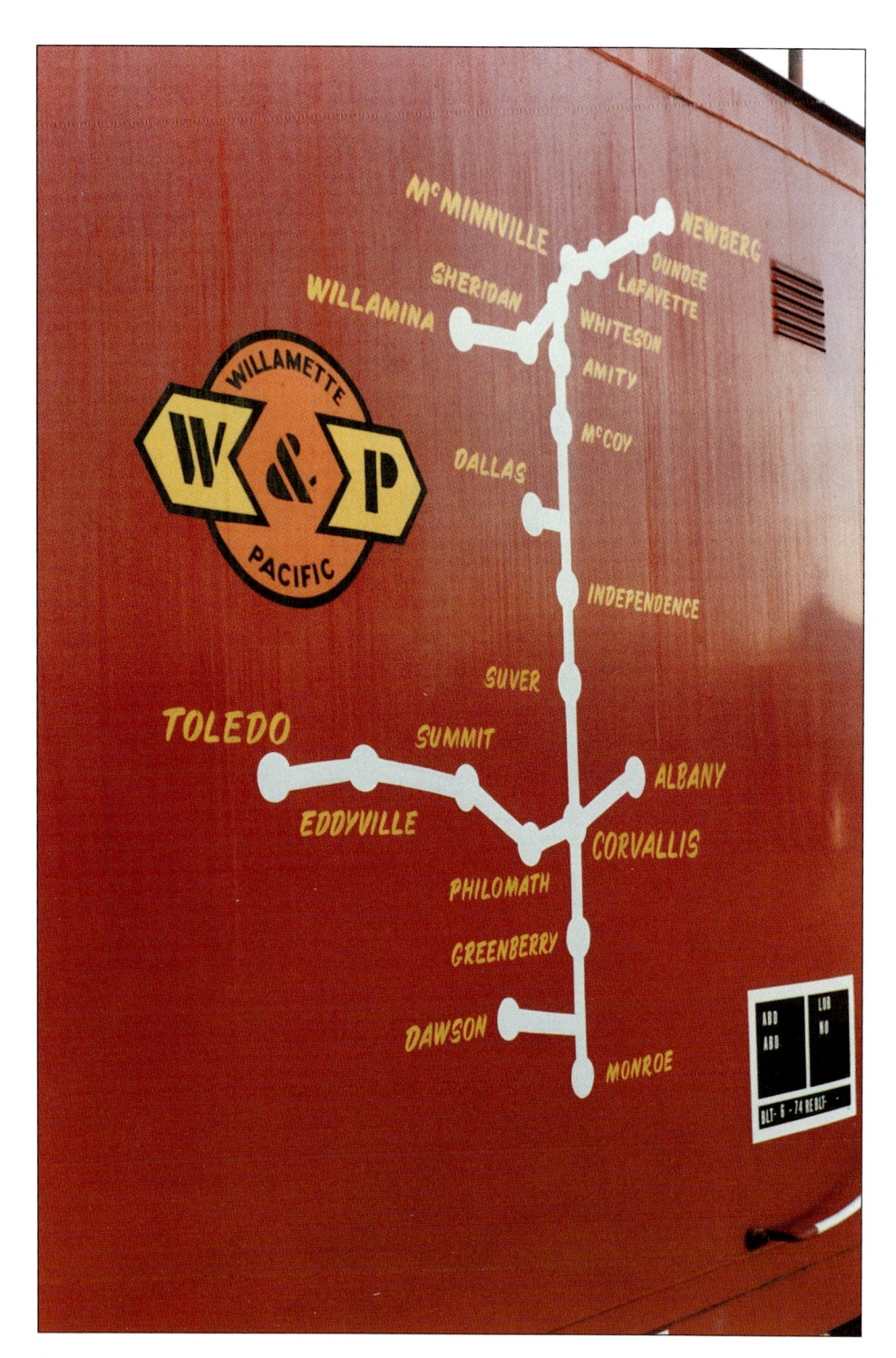

"CABOOSE MAP"
Willamette & Pacific Railroad
W&P #02
Hillsboro, Oregon
March 1995

"SERVING OREGON'S HEARTLAND" ▶
Willamette & Pacific Railroad
GP9 #1803
Dallas District
Gerlinger Junction, Oregon
August 1, 1996

The Willamette & Pacific Railroad brought some bright colors to the Oregon countryside when it replaced Southern Pacific operations on several branches in 1993. W&P also assigned names to its locomotives, something not seen on SP. At Gerlinger Junction, Oregon, on August 1, 1996 — in the middle of field-burning season — W&P GP9 #1803, "Sherwood," awaits a crew. The unit is parked, along with a few freight cars, next to a seemingly endless wheat field on part of what remains of the former SP Dallas Branch. The isolated junction was named for Louis Gerlinger, who created the Salem, Falls City & Western Railway, which later became part of the Southern Pacific empire.

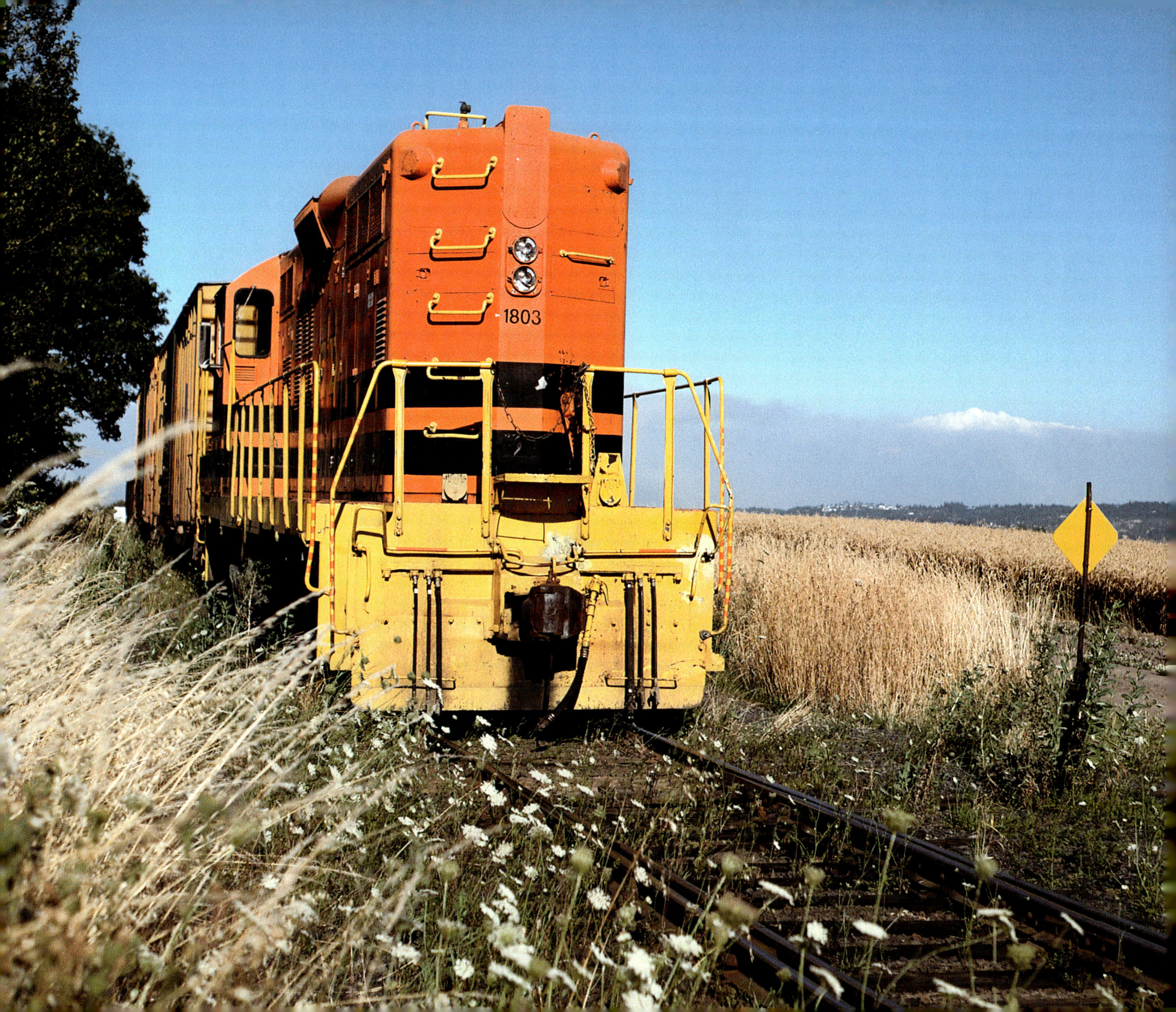
1803

Southern Pacific's Coos Bay Hauler is lost in the scenic landscape as it rolls through Gardiner Junction, Oregon, on July 26, 1993. Three Southern Pacific SD9s provide power on a train of gondolas, boxcars, and flatcars headed toward Coos Bay. The recently-logged hills behind the train demonstrate that Oregon's economy — along with many of its railroads — remains largely lumber-dependent. The Central Oregon & Pacific Railroad took over service on the Coos Bay Line on December 31, 1994.

"LUMBER ECONOMY"
Southern Pacific Railroad
Coos Bay Branch
Gardiner Junction, Oregon
July 26, 1993

"UMPQUA CROSSING"
Southern Pacific Railroad
SD9 #4424/SD9 #4396/SD9 #4423/GP9 #3840
Coos Bay Line
East Gardiner, Oregon
June 19, 1990

"HOLDING TO TRADITION"
Southern Pacific Railroad
Coos Bay Branch
Reedsport, Oregon
June 19, 1990

The tail of Southern Pacific's Coos Bay Hauler, with a Cotton Belt bay-window waycar (SSW #65) at the rear, slips across a fill over coastal marshlands directly north of the Umpqua River and Reedsport, Oregon. The head end of this train has already reached Gardiner Junction, interchange point with the Longview, Portland & Northern Railway. The cars pictured in this idyllic scene from June 1990 provide a clue as to the primary commodities moving over the Coos Bay Line — almost entirely lumber products and liquefied petroleum gas. Cabooses will probably never again be seen on the line.

"COAST RANGE CLIMB"

Spirit of Oregon
Alco C415s #701 and #702
Tillamook Branch
Scofield, Oregon
September 4, 1993

The Spirit of Oregon *dinner train comes through heavy forest cover in the foothills of the Coast Range Mountains near Scofield, Oregon, in September 1993. The two Alco C415s pulling the four-car train are former Columbia & Cowlitz Railway units, which entrepreneur Bob Steele purchased in 1988. After refurbishing and repainting the locomotives, Steele used them to power the dinner trains, which ran between Roy and Cochran, on the eastern end of the Port of Tillamook Bay Railroad's ex-SP Tillamook Branch. The inaugural run was on February 14, 1993 — Valentine's Day. Steele's* Spirit of Oregon *trains stopped running in August 1996, and the company subsequently went out of business. The dinner train was leased to the Mount Hood Railroad in March 1997, and began service between Hood River and Parkdale on April 19, 1997.*

"LOCAL WAIT"
Burlington Northern Santa Fe Railway
Astoria Branch
St. Helens, Oregon
October 1996

> ❝ *The trackside milieu is a secret universe, preserved outside of time. Railroad space creates its own kind of outlaw landscape of fringe neighborhoods, flourishing along the unheeded routes where nature, never quite extinguished, comes creeping back into town.* ❞
>
> — Michael Flanagan, *"Stations: An Imagined Journey,"* 1994

III. The Unheeded Routes: Northwest Images

The evolution of the Northwest's railroad industry was tied closely to the decisions of the major interstate carriers. When lines were under consideration for abandonment, entrepreneurs often moved in to try to keep lightly-trafficked routes going. Regional carriers and shortlines were born as SP, BN, and UP retrenched.

Through necessity, the shortlines proved adept at livening the often monochromatic railroad landscape. As they generally couldn't afford to purchase new locomotives or freight cars, the shortlines bought them used, or leased them from the big players. This served to provide a sometimes outlandish panoply of images. Unusual paint combinations on backwater freight lines exhibited an eclectic mix of rag-tag older models.

Some rail carriers appeared to be just hanging on, keeping marginal routes alive. Images of the changing transportation realities in the Northwest revealed a system with rough edges: marginal perhaps, but definitely charming ...

"SCRAP LINE"
Weyerhaeuser Company
Springfield, Oregon
July 19, 1988

Into the late 1980s, Weyerhaeuser operated a logging railroad that tapped timber resources in the hills around its massive mill at Springfield, Oregon. The rail line went north from the Weyerhaeuser facility and came to an end outside of Marcola, about 16 miles away. Trains ran on a regular weekday basis, but log train operations ended in the late 1980s as the timber supply ran low in the area. Weyerhaeuser then began the process of liquidating its railroad assets — in this case, the spine flats. The steel wheels were sold for scrap, as were most of the flatcars, although a few ended up on other Weyerhaeuser lines in the United States. The route to Marcola was abandoned a few months after this scene was recorded in July 1988.

Battered and weather-beaten but still serving, Burlington Northern GP9 #1812 moves through Vancouver, Washington, in February 1995. The locomotive was built by General Motors' Electro-Motive Division in the mid-1950s.

"AIN'T IT PRETTY"
Burlington Northern Railroad
GP9 #1812
Seattle Subdivision
Vancouver, Washington
February 25, 1995

61

"DAYLIGHT IN THE CASCADES"

Southern Pacific Railroad
SP #4449
Cascade Line
Dougren, Oregon
June 1989

Southern Pacific 4-8-4 locomotive #4449 glides south through Dougren, Oregon, on SP's Cascade Line, in June 1989. The steam locomotive — one of 50 of its type ordered by SP in the late 1930s and early 1940s — was on its way from Portland to Los Angeles to celebrate the 50th anniversary of LA's Union Station. These locomotives were used to pull SP's passenger trains, including the famous "Daylight" trains that operated along the California coast. SP #4449 was built in 1941 by Lima Locomotive Works in Lima, Ohio. It was retired on October 2, 1957, at Bakersfield, California, but was later restored to service as part of the 1976 Bicentennial celebration.

"LEFT HANGING"
Tacoma Eastern Railway
3rd Subdivision
Centralia, Washington
April 20, 1996

Looking south on the Tacoma Eastern Railway at Centralia, Washington, in April 1996. Raging floodwaters in February of that year were severe enough to rip away this steel trestle, leaving the rails hanging over the Chehalis River. As a result of the damage, a short section of the 54-mile line from Chehalis to Frederickson — formerly belonging to the Chehalis Western Railroad, and before that the Milwaukee Road — was out of service for well over a year. The bridge was scheduled to be repaired by late 1997, with financial help coming from the Federal Emergency Management Agency.

A series of Union Pacific boxcars built in the early 1970s featured this colorful logo and slogan. A quarter of a century later, after countless hours in snow, rain, and sunshine, the colors are fading and the paint is cracking, and most of these cars have been taken out of revenue service. This one, UP #917126, was in a corner of UP's freight yard at Pendleton, Oregon, being used for tool storage by a maintenance of way gang.

"AUTOMATED RAIL"
Union Pacific Railroad
UP #917126
La Grande Subdivision
Pendleton, Oregon
April 1997

64

"SEAMLESS SERVICE"

Burlington Northern Santa Fe Railway
Oregon Trunk Subdivision
Deschutes River Canyon
Moody, Oregon
May 1997

A northbound (eastward by railroad timetable) mixed merchandise train led by BN GP50 #3137 glides through Moody, Oregon, on the Oregon Trunk Subdivision on a hot day in May 1997. That same month, Burlington Northern Santa Fe and Union Pacific finalized an agreement that conveyed 112 miles of UP trackage in northern California to BNSF, thus extending the southern reach of the Oregon Trunk. Adding the "Inside Gateway" route between Keddie and Bieber, California, provided BNSF with direct single-line service in the Vancouver, British Columbia-San Diego, California corridor. UP's sale of the track segment was one of the conditions imposed by the Surface Transportation Board when it approved the Union Pacific/Southern Pacific merger in 1996. The transaction, which cost BNSF $30 million, became official on May 23, 1997.

"OAKBROOK MIX"
Burlington Northern Santa Fe Railway
Oregon Trunk Subdivision
Deschutes River Canyon
Oakbrook, Oregon
May 28, 1997

A southbound container train rolls onto the siding at Oakbrook, Oregon, on BNSF's Oregon Trunk Subdivision. Three units — BN SD40-2 #7158, LMX B39-8 #8562, and Santa Fe GP35 #2920 — power the trainload of all empties through the awesome Deschutes River Canyon. The train is taking the siding to await a northbound mixed manifest train bound for Wishram, Washington.

▶ "SHERARS CROSSING"
Burlington Northern Santa Fe Railway
Oregon Trunk Subdivision
Deschutes River Canyon
Sherars Bridge, Oregon
May 28, 1997

Almost a mile behind the three units on the head end, a lonely caboose trails the southbound container train, as BN #12332 rolls across a trestle over the Deschutes River at Sherar, Oregon. Cabooses are still used on this line to expedite switching at sidings, as most of the switches on the Oregon Trunk Line need to be opened and closed by hand.

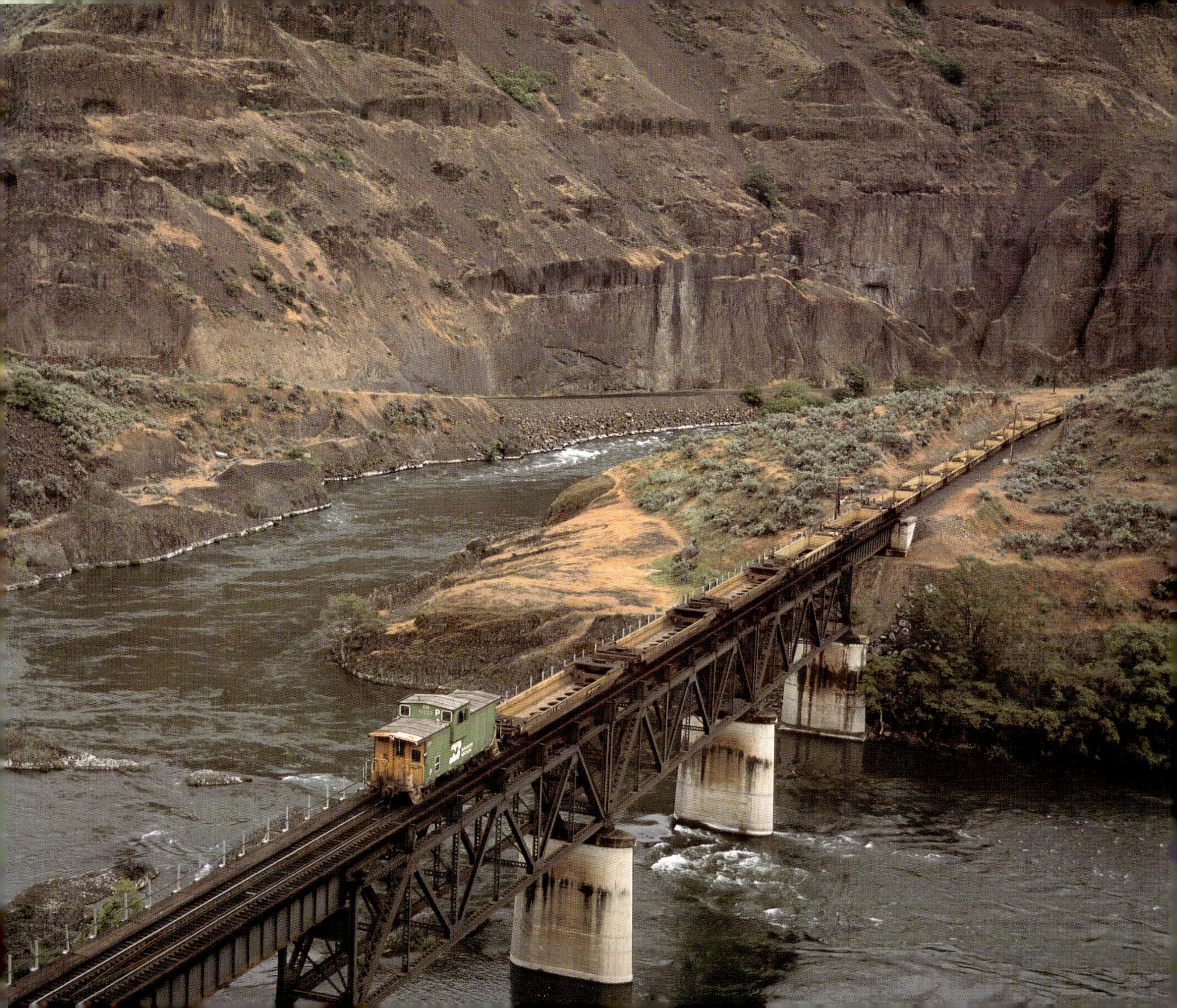
BN
P

"WARNER MOUNTAINS"
Southern Pacific Railroad
Modoc Line
Likely, California
August 3, 1996

An eastbound Southern Pacific freight snakes its way up the grade of the Warner Mountains, just south of Likely, California, on SP's Modoc Line. The heavy train out of Klamath Falls, Oregon, rates a total of eight locomotives, including a four-unit helper set near the middle of the train.

Under threatening skies, a hand-fashioned signpost points the way to Flanigan, Nevada, near where Southern Pacific's Modoc Line joins Union Pacific's former Western Pacific mainline between Oakland and Salt Lake City. The ominous desert sky seems appropriate: the date is May 24, 1996, and if Union Pacific's merger plans with SP are realized, SP's magnificent Modoc Line may soon be lost.

"HAND-PAINTED"
SP Modoc Subdivision
UP Elko Subdivision
Flanigan, Nevada
May 24, 1996

"MODOC POWER"
Southern Pacific Railroad
Modoc Line
Madeline, California
August 3, 1996

Coming out of the mountains, the train heads through relatively flat scrub-brush country near Madeline, California, as it continues on its eastward journey toward Ogden, Utah, behind a mixture of power: SP SD40T-2 #8360, SP SD45T-2 #7411, SP SD40-2 #7308, and SP SD40-2 #7380.

"DUSTY ARRIVAL"

Burlington Northern Santa Fe Railway
Wishram Subdivision
Wishram, Washington
August 1996

An eastbound train has just pulled into Burlington Northern Santa Fe's freight yard at Wishram, Washington, at dusk on a calm August evening. Their day's work completed, the crew is awaiting the arrival of the speeding shuttle vehicle that will carry them back to the depot.

"SURPRISE VISITOR"
Nickel Plate Road
Alco RS3 #324
Banks, Oregon
March 29, 1996

After flooding in February 1996 washed out sections of the Port of Tillamook Bay Railroad line to Tillamook — stranding most of the shortline's locomotives, along with approximately 60 freight cars — the POTB needed help to continue to serve its customers on the eastern end of its territory. Alco RS3 #324, in Nickel Plate Road livery, rests in Banks, Oregon, ready to serve. The unit, previously on the Utah Railway's roster, was on lease from a private owner, Doyle McCormack, who lives in Oregon City, Oregon. McCormack, who once lived in the old Nickel Plate Road's territory, painted his engine accordingly.

"HAULER TAIL"
Southern Pacific Railroad
D&RGW #01457
Toledo Hauler
Albany, Oregon
January 10, 1990

An unusual assortment of cabooses showed up on Southern Pacific's Toledo Hauler in the early 1990s, including some from Soo Line and Burlington Northern. In this scene from January 10, 1990, Denver & Rio Grande Western caboose #01457 is on the tail of the westbound Toledo Hauler, framed by the joint SP/Amtrak depot at Albany, Oregon.

"PARTNERSHIP IN GRAIN"
Blue Mountain Railroad
The Dalles, Oregon
May 1997

Twenty-five hoppers — almost the entire fleet of the Blue Mountain Railroad's colorful "Grain Train" cars — are lined up in the Union Pacific freight yard at The Dalles, Oregon, in the spring of 1997. In partnership with the Blue Mountain Railroad and the Port of Walla Walla, the Washington State Energy Office and the Washington Department of Transportation provided funding to purchase 29 used grain hoppers in 1994. Wheat production is one of Washington's biggest industries, so the state helped cover the cost of refurbishing the cars in an effort designed to reduce shipping costs for grain producers; reduce truck use on rural Washington roads; and provide enough freight cars to move grain efficiently. Rural Northwest shippers — particulary in southeast Washington, where the Blue Mountain Railroad operates — often have experienced car supply difficulties.

"GHOST OF THE ROCK"
C&NW #717061
Bingen, Washington
April 1995

An ex-Rock Island Railroad boxcar stands out against the sky, the puffy clouds, and the bluffs around Bingen, Washington. Chicago & NorthWestern bought dozens of these boxcars after the Rock Island ceased operations in 1980. C&NW painted over the defunct carrier's logos and slogans on many of the boxcars, but on this one only the lettering and serial number was changed: from ROCK #300655 to C&NW #717061. The growing streaks of rust reflect the car's age, but nevertheless the weathered paint keeps the vanishing image of a historic Midwestern carrier alive a little longer.

"25 LIMIT"
Snoqualmie Valley Railroad
North Bend, Washington
May 1996

"CANYON LINE"
Union Pacific Railroad
Bend Branch
Deschutes River Canyon
June 1, 1996

Union Pacific's Bend Local rolls north through the Deschutes River Canyon on Burlington Northern Santa Fe's Oregon Trunk Line, headed toward The Dalles, Oregon. The local operates between The Dalles and Bend six days a week, normally using a two-unit set of GP38-2s, as is the case on this run, with #2033 and #2038 doing the work. UP operates on this BN route courtesy of a long-standing trackage rights agreement.

"TRACKAGE RIGHTS" ▶
Union Pacific Railroad
Bend Branch
Deschutes River Canyon
Moody, Oregon
June 1, 1996

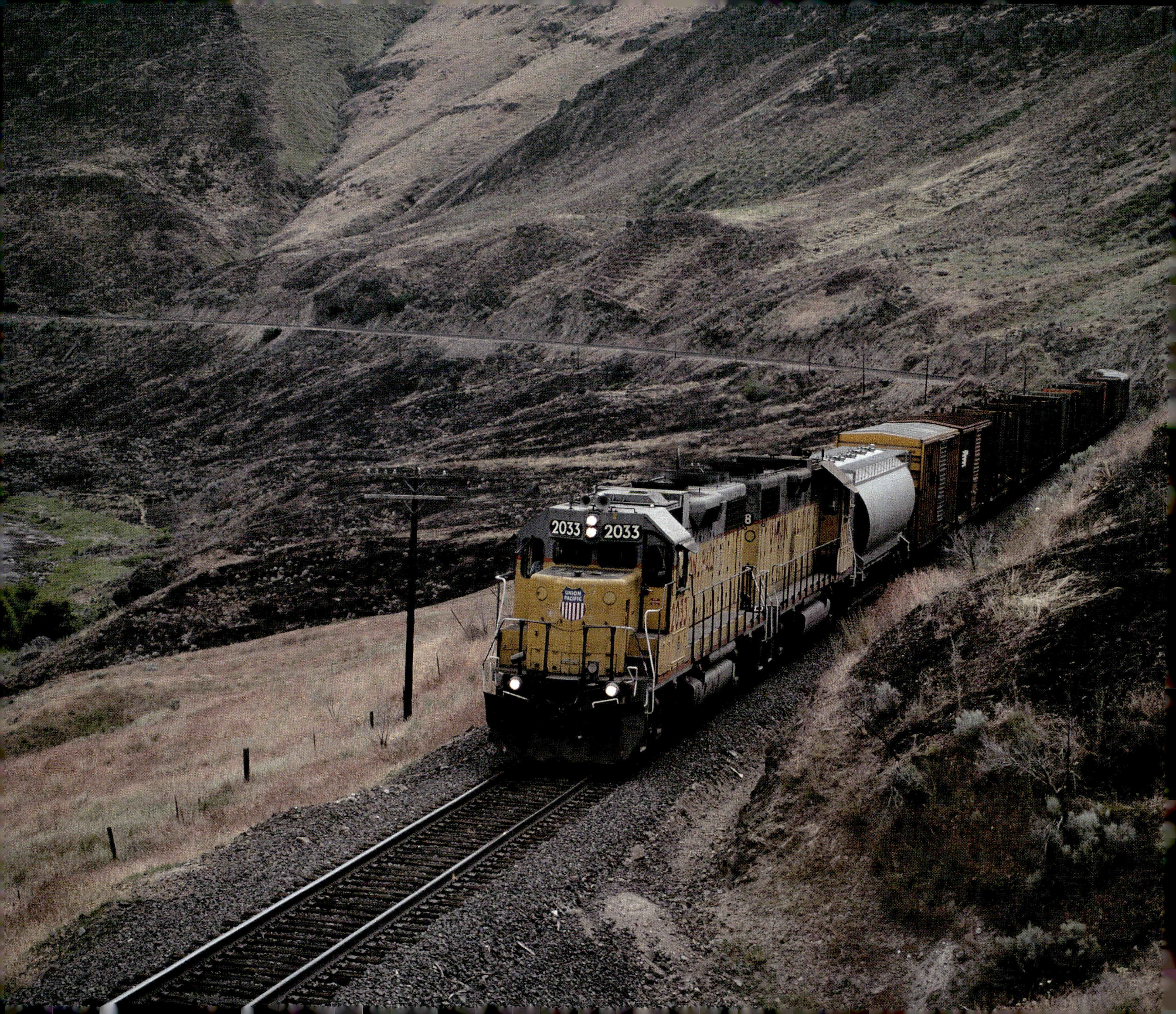
2033
2033

"GO BY TRAIN"
Union Station
Portland, Oregon
July 1993

"AMTRAK FACE"
F40PH #401
Union Station
Portland, Oregon
July 1993

Denver & Rio Grande Western SD40T-2 #5390 and Southern Pacific SD45T-2 #7410 roll along beside an Amtrak train stopped at Portland's Union Station. The historic Rio Grande (once billed as the "Scenic Line of the World") image is rapidly vanishing from the Western landscape. Southern Pacific and Rio Grande joined forces in August 1988, when Rio Grande Industries purchased Southern Pacific for $1.8 billion; then the Rio Grande was further submerged when Union Pacific swallowed SP/D&RGW in 1996.

"SCENIC LINE"
Denver & Rio Grande Western Railroad
D&RGW SD40T-2 #5390/SP SD45T-2 #7410
Portland, Oregon
September 1995

"WORKHORSE"

Burlington Northern Railroad
SD9 #6145
Oregon Trunk Subdivision
Klamath Falls, Oregon
May 23, 1996

Pouring out heavy black smoke, a workhorse switching locomotive bangs cars around Burlington Northern's busy yard in Klamath Falls, Oregon, at a little after 7 p.m. on May 23, 1996. The unit is an SD9, a type that is relatively uncommon on BN lines in the Pacific Northwest. Although dozens of them were built between 1954 and 1959 by predecessor carriers, most of the SD9s BN inherited ended up in service on other parts of its system.

"THE RIGHT TOOL FOR THE JOB"
Burlington Northern Railroad
Tunnel #3
Fallbridge Subdivision
Cooks, Washington
April 22, 1995

❝ *The color scheme of yards is done in pastels, and these colors seem to be subdued by a thin layer of soot. The tops of the rails are bright, a penetrating silver that gleams in the sunlight and reflects lanterns and engine headlights at night. As they move the reflections scurry ahead of them on the rails. All else is muted in tone: the rusty sides of the tracks, the rocks on the roadbed, the dusty engines and cars, some once bright but now toned down by diesel and city smoke.* ❞

— Michael Mathers, *"Riding the Rails,"* 1973

IV. Done in Pastels: Dispatches

The following is the author's on-scene news account and photography of a bizarre wreck that took place on April 22, 1995, while he served as editor of The Enterprise, *a weekly newspaper in White Salmon, Washington. The report is as it appeared in the newspaper.*

"Incident At MP 68"

COOKS, Wash. — Along the Washington side of the Columbia River, the east-west mainline of Burlington Northern Railroad parallels Washington's Route 14 in many places. Sometimes it's almost close enough to reach out and touch.

On April 22, at 8:34 a.m., Francis Greiner, 38, of Portland, Oregon, was traveling westbound alongside one of those side-by-side stretches when he fell asleep behind the wheel of a 24-foot Ford U-Haul trailer. Greiner's empty truck swerved off the road, roared up the paralleling railroad embankment and sailed into the air.

When it came down, it slid on its side — not on asphalt any longer, but instead on the twin steel rails of Burlington Northern's Fallbridge Subdivision mainline. The concrete face of BN's Tunnel #3 jolted the U-Haul truck to a sudden halt, smashing the windshield and leaving the truck pressed against the mouth of the railroad tunnel. It was resting passenger side down, with its wheels facing west.

The truck was only a few feet from railroad Milepost 68, completely blocking the eastern portal of a tunnel on a transcontinental line that hosts approximately 30 trains a day.

Greiner somehow got out of the truck and began walking around in a daze inside the dark tunnel. Blood was coming from a wound to his head. A hunter camping in the area heard the sound of the truck's impact with the tunnel and ran to the scene and began yelling at Greiner to get out of the tunnel in case a train was coming.

Five miles to the east, BN engineer Leon Batanian, 42, was guiding BN Train G-87, a contract grain train hauling 13,000 tons toward Vancouver. The train, out of Pasco, was already west of Bingen and coming out of a 25 mph speed zone. Batanian was preparing to accelerate to 45 mph. As his long freight train rumbled westbound toward the wreck, a signal flashed from green to red directly in front of the train.

"When a circuit gets fouled, the signal goes red," Batanian explained. Batanian, who lives in Vancouver, understood how close he had come to possibly derailing his train; to possibly killing someone. Even at 25 mph, it took Batanian half a mile to get the train stopped.

The BN dispatcher, meanwhile, informed the train crew that he had been advised there was a moving van stuck in the tunnel ahead, and gave the engineer permission to proceed at restricted speed, meaning slow enough that he could stop short of any track blockage. Batanian halted the train a couple hundred yards short of the wreck, then walked up to have a closer look.

"Five minutes later and we would have been running on a clear signal at 45 mph," he said. "We would have punched him clear through the tunnel. At 45 mph, we would have gone through him like butter."

Batanian said he had 17 years of experience as an engineer — with Santa Fe, Amtrak, and Burlington Northern — and in all that time had never hit anyone.

"I've seen some odd stuff, but never anything like that before — not where someone got stuck in a tunnel," Batanian added in amazement.

Batanian said he thought he probably would have seen the truck blocking the tunnel perhaps as much as half a mile away, but even that would not have been soon enough to prevent a collision. He added that he would have put the train in "emergency" immediately, but knew he could have derailed the train in the process.

"You try to stop consistent with good train handling," he said. "But you can get poor slack action and derail the train."

A tow truck came from nearby White Salmon to clear the wrecked U-Haul, but its cables and winches were not enough to pull the truck out. It was wedged in tight.

"I can't understand how he got that truck in that position," said Bob Baker, owner of the towing company. "He took a heck of a bounce. He must have been going like crazy."

"He ruined a good day for us," Batanian joked. "We were going to get in early until that. You just can't put a square peg in a round hole."

After seeing that the tow truck wasn't going to be able to clear the van from the tracks, Batanian asked the section crew that had come over from Bingen if they wanted him to use the train's locomotives to pull the truck out of the way. They said they did, so Batanian brought up his units: BN SD40-2 #8083, BN B30-7AB (cabless) #4039, Montana Rail Link SD40 #221, and leased Electro-Motive Division SD40 #6043.

The track crew hooked cables to the smashed truck, and Batanian edged the locomotives back, pulling the truck onto its wheels.

"We couldn't even feel it," Batanian said. "We had 12,000 horsepower — four 3,000 horsepower units. I'm just glad the guy's all right, that's the main thing."

"It makes for an exciting day," added conductor Teresa Hamann. "It was boring before this."

The tracks were undamaged in the accident, and by 10 a.m., trains were rolling again, with Batanian's grain train, appropriately, rolling first through the cleared tunnel.

The Washington State Patrol cited Greiner for reckless driving. "He hadn't had enough rest and admitted he was pushing it," said WSP Trooper Mark Hirz. "That was an unusual accident. He was lucky to escape."

Greiner was treated by medics on the scene. Miraculously, he was not seriously hurt, although the rented U-Haul suffered an estimated $10,000 in damage.

Standing alongside the highway, blood welling up on his forehead, Greiner somehow retained his sense of humor.

"I was just going over there to park," he joked.

# # #

"SURVIVOR"
Tuscola & Saginaw Bay Railroad
TSBY GP35 #390
Manton, Michigan
October 1992

❝ I was going to open the door and just look inside, but she stopped me. 'Don't do that,' she said. 'You might let the outside in.' ❞

— Carlos Castaneda, *"The Art of Dreaming,"* 1993

In October 1992, a three-car Tuscola & Saginaw Bay Railroad local rolls southbound through Manton, Michigan, on former Penn Central (ex-Pennsylvania Railroad) track. Pulling the train through the light snowscape is ex-Ann Arbor Railroad GP35 #390, a survivor of Michigan's railroad wars. The train is on its way from Traverse City to Cadillac. The TSBY usually serves shippers on this stretch of track twice a week.

V. Addendum: Michigan Roots

The railroad systems of Oregon and Michigan share a number of similarities. Both systems were built primarily to tap what at one time seemed like endless forests. Both states have suffered — albeit in different decades and in different ways — with the decline of key industries.

And both states are witnessing the creation of new shortlines that have sprung up from the ashes of large carriers (e.g., Southern Pacific in Oregon; Penn Central in Michigan) that couldn't adapt quickly enough to survive intact . . .

"AUTUMN CHANGES"
Ann Arbor Railroad
Elberta, Michigan
October 1992

Until the early 1980s, the Ann Arbor Railroad's 292-mile mainline carried long, daily freight trains between Toledo, Ohio, and Elberta, Michigan, on the northwestern shore of Lake Michigan. But with the April 1982 termination of the railroad's carferry service across Lake Michigan to Wisconsin points, service slowed, then finally halted. In a scene from 1992, the Ann Arbor Railroad's tracks — out of service for several years — vanish into the autumn weeds a few miles east of Elberta.

Special Thanks List:

"BLUE NORTHERN"
Great Northern Railway
Extra #2542 East
Harrington, Washington
February 28, 1970
Photo by Dale Jones

Gus Melonas: Burlington Northern Santa Fe Railway
Ed Trandahl: Union Pacific Railroad
Micki Chapman: Graphic design; patience with alterations
John Mausen: Wy'east Color Labs
Bob Dobyne: Mirror Image Photo Lab, The Dalles
Bob Melbo: Willamette & Pacific Railroad
David Root: Willamette Valley Railroad
Dick Samuels: Oregon Pacific Railroad
Dave Sprau: Tacoma Eastern Railway
Bob and Vickie Steele: *Spirit of Oregon*
Ed Immel: Oregon Department of Transportation
Roy Hill: City of Prineville Railway
Steve Kahler: Blue Mountain Railroad
Terry Anderson: Klamath Northern Railway
Walt Brickwedel: Central Oregon & Pacific Railroad
Leon Batanian: BNSF engineer, Tunnel #3

Leslie Ann Jackson Hennelly: *Self-Publishing Manual*; plant identifications
Thomas J. Lacinski: Author photo; Flaming Gorge; Manton, Michigan
Paulette K. Pollard: Sherars Bridge and Stronghold; keying "Dispatches"
Louise Moore: Dynagraphics
Rob Carlson: Rail map; Altamont Press timetables
Lowell Smith: Portland "N" connection
Elaine Bakke: *Enterprise* ads; fresh salsa
Chris Jaques: BNSF colors; awards in Pasco, Yakima
Tom Dill: SP loyalist; "Turntable" photo
Ronald R. Burkhardt: The surf at Laguna Beach
Christopher T. Burkhardt: Boxcar money
Dale Jones: Great Northern imagery, 1970
Scott Sparling: the Penn Central line to Elkhart; Earle at Champoeg
Robert and Lois Burkhardt: Passenger trains, Jackson depot
Pentax K-1000 cameras

You go great when you go
Great Northern

85

"JACKSON BREAK"
D. C. Jesse Burkhardt
Jackson, Wyoming
August 1994
Photo by Thomas J. Lacinski